PARABLE ISLAND

Books by Pauline Stainer

Little Egypt (Smith/Doorstop Books, 1987)

The Honeycomb (Bloodaxe Books, 1989)
WITH ILLUSTRATIONS BY BRIAN PARTRIDGE

Sighting the Slave Ship (Bloodaxe Books, 1992)

The Ice-Pilot Speaks (Bloodaxe Books, 1994)

The No-Man's Tree (MakingWaves, 1994)
SELECTED POEMS TRANSLATED FROM THE NORWEGIAN
BY ÅSE-MARIE NESSE AND PAULINE STAINER

Salt over Skara Brae (Prospero Poets, 1995)
WITH ILLUSTRATIONS BY JOSEPH HEWES

The Wound-dresser's Dream (Bloodaxe Books, 1996)

Parable Island (Bloodaxe Books, 1999)

PARABLE ISLAND

PAULINE STAINER

BLOODAXE BOOKS

ISBN: 1 85224 501 8

First published 1999 by
Bloodaxe Books Ltd,
P.O. Box 1SN,
Newcastle upon Tyne NE99 1SN

Bloodaxe Books Ltd acknowledges
the financial assistance of Northern Arts.

Cover printing by J. Thomson Colour Printers Ltd, Glasgow.

Printed in Great Britain by
Cromwell Press Ltd, Trowbridge, Wiltshire.

for Beatrice and Donald

Acknowledgements

Acknowledgements are due to the editors of the following publications where some of these poems first appeared: *Acumen, Atlanta Review, The Frogmore Papers, The Green Book, Kunapipi, Last Words* (Picador, 1999), *New Blood* (Bloodaxe Books, 1999), *Notre Dame Review, Odyssey, Orkney Arts Review, Other Poetry, Poetry London, Poetry Quarterly Review, Poetry Review, The Rialto, Scintilla, The Tabla Book of New Verse* (1999), *Thames* (Enitharmon Press, 1999), *Stand* and *Unknown Public.*

The sequence *Salt over Skara Brae* was first published by Prospero Poets in 1995, with illustrations by Joseph Hewes, and *Little Egypt* by Smith/Doorstop Books in 1987. 'Potosí' was a winning poem in the *TLS*/Poetry on the Underground competition in 1996 and appears in the Anniversary Edition of *Poems on the Underground* (Cassell, 1996). 'The snake-dancer' was commissioned by the Salisbury Festival's Last Words, 1999.

Contents

You know, however long I live I shall remember
the middle watch. I shall think of it as a kind of
– island – out of this world – made of moonlight –
– WILLIAM GOLDING

Footfalls

They came softly
into the underground chamber –
cave-divers
working by touch alone.

They found no red ochre,
no handprints,
only wolf-bones
and small footsteps in the mud.

Such clear heelmarks
showed the children
had been in no hurry
three thousand years earlier

but the divers never forgot
the racing
of their luminous watch-dials
as they heard

footfalls
(sole-sizes eight and eleven)
steal away
over the younger gravels.

Within North

A body on a sheet
of birchbark
in the acid peat,
an armband of foxfur,
vulpes vulpes
fluorescing bright green
in ultraviolet light.

The dead are masters
of diminishing return

but I still see her –
the dancer
with the antler head-dress,
binding her breasts
at the burial
of a stillborn child
to stop the milk rising.

Listening-in

Even flint-scatter
is a manner of speaking
and there is no whisper
like that of the stone axe
in its antler sleeve.

As for the dead,
their applied energy
still catches the light
in the horizontal hail
like salt on the lips.

Sourin

I

Read it simply:
the hawk as outbreath,
the sleeve of the wind
engraved with cloud-forms,
dusk unlatching its blues

and on the shingle
before the driftwood cross,
the priest lifting the word
against a fetch of shining water
as if the light had uttered.

II

The poetry is not firstly in the words;
a bright moon
holds shoals to the sea-bed

salt bruises the rose
to the vibration of a magical string
without sound.

III

How it glitters – the haul
between ebb and incoming

arctic terns fencing with mirrors
between the islands

the drowned pressing spindrift
to their faces
like little veronicas.

IV

The island makes its own cloud,
a soft drum-roll
kid-covered

a swan hangs
from the power-lines,
Odin realises the runes

and the imprint
of snow on water
says next to nothing.

Prima Nix

(for the nuns of Fetlar)

First snow
not yet dashed with a hare's foot.
We could go to our graves in white
not dead
but simply listening.

A simple interior,
the sound of the sea
through snowfall,
a cross-shaped cut in the membrane
behind the lens.

Prayer without words;
where the light meets the water
great areas left
unprinted
like a Japanese rice-paper painting.

Salt settles on the skin.
The ghostly disciples let
their heads fall forward
in the wind
like melancholy thistles.

Our Lady of the Isles
all the blues swallow one another.
Christ colours the quickbread.
The islands glide
into one body.

Blodeuwedd in Orkney

'And even now the owl is called Blodeuwedd.'

I have seen her hunt
at midsummer
when the night shines
as the day.

How can she
hide her face
in the glitter of salt
off the glass-green graves?

How can she hide
on white nights
the complicated reds
of the heart?

Wyre

Time was a falconer's knot
tied and untied with one hand

the island wearing a yellow tippet,
the midden blue-steaming into the sun

fish and shadow
under their glass roundel

and through the sea-door,
sailors, standing watch

as if the ice-bound ship
still moved.

Eynhallow

Hartstongue,
an absence of squirrels,
the rip-tide glistening
like a single muscle

smallpox
and cabin-fever,
a merlin's eye
as the sun and moon

the insolence of zero –
in Christ's wounds
the sea-swallow
purchasing a nest.

The Fall

That autumn
there was a fall of goldcrests
on the island.

They came through spindrift
like winnowed grain,
wave after wave

exhausted, silent,
thicker than leaves
on the rigging in North Bay

not even the burn of them
off the water
between midnight and morning.

And when the haar rose
from the shrouds
they were gone

migrating very fast
over slow shipwrecks
into the sun.

Harbour and Room

We read each other
with fingertips
in the white night

the still of the room
under the salt rafters
would turn us to dust

but outside,
like mercury, the water
runs without feet.

Thomas Vaughan experiments with mercury

Always dangerous –
the water of the moon
in a mutable glass.

Was it vapour
or the heavy shining oxides
of yellow and red?

The pure *solutio*
when death came running
without feet

glass billowing
in the blast,
the birds outside

shaking metallic wings
as after rain.

St Brendan's birds

Not Sigurd's nuthatches
clattering in the brush,
but diamond vehicles,
their ribcages sprung with light
as they sing
the eight canonical hours

passerines,
weightless after migration –
magnetic particles
of iron oxide
in their retinas –
spirits fired with blood

as on St Kilda,
where if you put your ear
to the carbon-dating,
you hear the wrens
settle like small rain
on the tree-rings.

St Kilda

I weigh the heavy pollen count
against an ounce of indigo
as the trees vanish.

The islanders wear disposable shoes:
gannet-necks, slit from eye to breast,
feathered on the inside.

They salt-down the solan geese,
making their own blizzard,
guano giving a tincture to the sea.

In the blackhouses
there is the smell of silverweed, fulmar oil;
the babies have lockjaw

and from the end of the jetty,
eyes burning like millstones,
hark how the dogs do bark.

Lambholm

Here
at the salt edge of things,
the six-cornered snowflake
falls on simple moss.

Madonna of the Nissen huts –
your candles spit
before the creatures
of bread and wine

the sea reassembles its engines,
Italian prisoners of war
build the barriers
in a wolfish light

their prayers
tiny depressions
in the silence
like fossil raindrops.

Abseiling the waterfall

Mosses
shouldering one another
each side the double rope

a vein of satin spar

the imprint of a boot
suggesting silk-weave
on wet rock.

Moments
impacted under pressure,
marginal, imperious

the air full
of rapid asides,
and downstream

reflected boats
cubed by the ripple.

Mam Tor

We took the coffin-walk
in summer
from Edale to Castleton.

It was windless –
a farmer sharpening
his scythe
against the bloom
of the cement factory.

But I sensed
the slanting coffins
in the level sleet,
the whetstone singing
like a clouded jade

the quivered mountain
watching.

Bleaklow

They nearly made it –
the thirteen men
in the Superfortress.

The engines still crouch there
like animals
of the four directions.

We came up from the Roman road,
saw the sun
graze the fuselage

heard the dead sough
through the cylinder heads
they probably never saw the ground

and we lay there
like lovers
the earth not moving.

Little Egypt

1 *Sandpeople*

These are the sandpeople –
fixed by fugitive stain
in the acidic soil;
rayographs
on light-sensitive ground,
the real become the sign.

When we divested them
they lay north-south
in pagan burial;
encaustic, exemplary,
preparatory drawings
in silverpoint;

their insufficiency of bone
fluorescing
under ultra-violet,
an amber inclusion
still hung
at the striation of the throat.

No excavation
catches the slenderness
of their chance melting;
taking the first cast
we remembered those
from Pompeii

but later
seeing the half-profile
in fibreglass,
felt only
bright sufficiency
outstripping the bone.

Little Egypt is a local name for Sutton Hoo, the Viking burial-boat site in
Suffolk, as well as a name sometimes given to the Orkney island of Rousay,
which has many early tombs.

2 *Tide-mill near Sutton Hoo*

It wasn't the pull of the tide I felt,
but the pull of men
raising the funeral-ship on the far shore;

how they hauled the clinker-built boat
over the red crag
up through the bracken;

sited it stern seawards
on the spur,
sank the gunwale below the barrow.

Such cold inlay –
only armourers on an enamel field
to fix the dye in the heart.

But then the tide turned, the sluice opened,
the medieval mill-wheels ground
as they had for the Black Canons

and looking out across the flood,
I remembered the inventory
of the sacrificial vessel:

bronze stag, stone sceptre,
baptismal silver
for the blood thickening inshore –

and I sensed how they crossed –
kingship,
the occurrence of mercy

and that bright error of judgement
which made the Saxon bird
flash through the lighted hall.

3 *Little Egypt*

Here in wartime,
army recruits packed
the excavated ship with bracken,
drove a glider trench
between the barrows

oblivious of
the tilt of the burial-boat
in the battle-ditch,
the king pillowed
amidship
between the tholes of the gunwale.

Weapons furnish sacrifice;
those who forged the rivets
for the ribbed hull,
left vizor and neck-guard,
sword and helmet,
cheekpieces of iron.

Now American planes
rise and fall
above the spur of the land,
whilst far below
where the estuary widens
the tide – gunmetal grey –
rises in the reeds.

4 *The Dig*

They map out the mound
like surgeons
dividing a belly,
scan for echoes.

Here the stern
of the burial-boat
was removed by ploughing.

On this female grave,
they uncover the goosewing
with which she swept out the oven;
the worn spiral
of an ammonite
where her dress
once opened at the breast.

It is quirkish of time
to leave only a purposeful echo
among the erratics:

this male body
buried in ploughing-position
beside his plough,
the eager figure
bent forward over the coulter –
fragile, passionate,
as if still reining-in
the light.

5 *Iken*

It was here
they broke the ground
for the burial of a stranger;

gave him
high above the estuary
a silent riding at anchor.

In the roofless nave
where the floor is shingle,
only baptism troubles the water;

on the chancel altar
a bleeding-bowl
of alluvial silver.

Nothing furnishes us
for such ebbs
of extraordinary fall –

for whether the miraculous
draught of fishes
is water or light

for the angel
figured on the luminous strand
with instruments of passion.

The bright source
of sacrament
is the dispossession of wounds;

how piercing-strange
the severity of the rite,
the inconsequence of the tide.

The King's Candle-bearer

He lies easy:
the unsandalled spirit
of the king's candle-bearer.

He has run to green tallow
in the bladed sun
at the root of the tree.

Under the stone,
the radials of his hair
are ravelled with nettle-twine.

The spring, with her sorcerer's tongue,
has laced his mouth
with the red hawthorn.

He wears the pierced circle:
iron sword to magnetic north,
a torc round the vertebrae;

still holds a dim sconce:
lights the Host from his frost-pocket
with skeletal grace;

his solstice
the blessing of candles
on a ruinous place.

Double Portrait

(after Cecil Collins)

The artist and his wife
walk in a landscape,
he naked, she robed.

They dream the source:
seed and chrysalis,
the sprung-song of the tree

virgin images
in the magical processes
of time

and through the eye of the heart
angels are threshed
to the sound of the sea.

The Seals

There they were
at a solemn distance
like apostles

wedged
on white sand
in their skulking purples

the sea slung with weed
yet holding more light
than anything else.

Shaping spirits –
for when they had gone
we stood in the undertow

as if their music
were still perceived
through the skin.

And beyond the garden Gilgamesh saw the sea

At first, it was simply
a sense of gaze,
moonstone so smooth
he could have sculled across

then phosphorescence
where the fish spawn,
a shift of the shining reach
like a flute underblown

and beyond, rip-tides
flashing the sun,
the assuaging spices
on the salt-laden wind

specific as pollen.

The Stowaways

They stayed on the ship for years,
never giving an identity.

For what was time
when they went for months
without seeing land or darkness

swinging in bleached hammocks
between counterweights
of sun and moon?

But in dream
seal-women gave them molluscs
as they disembarked

and when they woke
the luminescence persisted
on their hands and mouths.

Between islands

Take her by the lily-white hand
Lead her across the water
Only memory
injects a tincture.

Indigo,
dusting the lagoon
where lepers once
stormed the pharmacy.

Parable Island

Cold midsummer
and the middle of nowhere –
salt on flint,
the light behaving as it does
between islands.

In the old fever-hospital,
sage and juniper,
the surgeon's kit
and his divining-rods
laid in the grave.

Tinctures multiply.
When the sea-mist
burns off at noon,
you could slip a blade
between the sea and the sky.

Against drowning

The surgeon uses coral
as substitute for bone

when suddenly they rise up –
the sailors of the *Mary Rose*

the billowed ends
of their longbones

still leaning into
their longbows.

Caravaggio

Round the piazza
the boy apprentices
lie lip to lip.

Pigments pool in the hot shade,
cinnabar and narcotic green
numb to the touch.

Yesterday I stabbed a man.
Today I grind vermilion
for the Madonna of the Rosary

the light a cardsharp
always a trick ahead.

Epiphany in Umbria

Driving between water and woodsmoke
I thought of St Francis:
how at a certain pitch, the sun
would strike both the stigmata
and the glass insulators
on the pylon.

Such melting abstracts –
all the while
the deer twinkling
their white underbellies
and looking like sunlight
before the sunlight hits them.

The Fallow Doe

It was she
who had caused the tail-back –
the rising vapour
not an overheated engine
but her breath
on the night air.

It still rives –
the way the exhaust
enhanced her aureole
as the engines idled,
she, heraldic in the headlights,
dying.

After Kosovo

Look across from Agni –
a mile and a half
over the water
Albania is in the sun.

Colours quicken
under the olive nets,
saffron crocus,
sea-squill and cyclamen

foxtail lilies
turning every way,
while far out
a shoal almost surfaces

subliminal red –
as if to reconcile
that impossible landfall
with the rippling dead.

Burning the Vixen

How they run –
the red oxides
down the white mountain
as the villagers
burn her

smoke rising
through the balsam poplars,
her straw limbs
winnowing

and higher still
above the threshing-circle,
death the skier
leaving the snow
red behind him.

The snake-dancer

is surrounded by a circle of ice,
glass-snakes coiled
on her head.

They pour down and sway,
mapping the warmth
of her body.

But that whisper – is it just
their skulls of fluid bone
grazing the ice

or *the desire of the line*,
melting, insatiable,
as the ice floats the sun?

Tracking down the twelve-wired bird of Paradise

(after Alfred Wallace)

It took years,
the journey to the interior –
and then the bird
a little less than a thrush.

So vivid, he thought
for a moment
he must have glimpsed it
with the mind's eye.

Its flight across
the synapses
metallic green,
deep cinnabar

and before memory
altered it,
the scent of ginger flowers
rising so whitely

he could have wintered
in their throats.

Coleridge in Malta

His daemons brought fire-flies
through green solar spectacles,
young lobsters, hauled up dripping,
their claws lapis-lazuli
against the light.

When the ship was the ripple
he drank the mirage –
red and yellow camphor trees
walking by
with their little fevers

the sun dropping molten shapes
into the sea,
the momentum of imagining
a fragment of gold foil
in a glass vacuum.

Hunting the geode

We dream of finding one
entire in the red rock

take the moonlight
as manna into our mouths

and leaning into the hot wind,
recall how the swallow heals

by casting a shadow.

Hoar-frost

It was like this
before language:
each tree striking
its triangle,
the eye backed with silver-leaf.

But we are weightless
after wintering
and can barely suffer
the hoar-frost
as ashes.

If poetry
is not firstly in the words
when will it become
again
prologue to the whole?

Finding the right blue for the waterfall
(for Roger Warr)

Hiroshige knew –

so solid a blue
the Victorian tight-rope walker
could have crossed
in the declining sun
without her white pole gleaming.

It's a metaphysical act,
intensifying the blue –
swallows in slow-motion,
stars perched on the overfall
without trepidation

as when Orpheus played.

Herman Melville jumps ship

They say that blue
slows the passage of time –
so what was
the blue reflex
when I jumped ship
at the Marquesas?

How was it I could read
by the blue light
from the *noctilucae*
but not look up at the vanishing ship
or the natives running like grass
before the wind?

Blondin

He couldn't see sunshine
at all, he said,
pulling huge crowds
at the Crystal Palace

the solid bubble
of the moon
on metal rails
in its blue-tinged box

as he crossed Niagara,
diabetic,
one blind eye
behind the blindfold.

Reading the Light

This is seriously old light;
we read it, like snow

cattle moving from bright pasture
to bright pasture

the sea wearing the ship's wake
like a firing scar;

a certain luminosity,
a simple kill

the tear of the gazelle
borrowing the light

like one of those shakes
in music

performed by a tremble
of the finger.

St Mary of Fountains

We came
and put on mortality
like a garment

under the Lady chapel
a skeleton with skull
placed on the breast.

St Mary of Fountains,
flowing physician –
which salve is which,

nakedness
where the heart was,
or your light off the water?

Revising the Three Crosses

(after Rembrandt)

What made you years later
burnish out
the kneeling centurion
as if anguish is always
beyond the exactitude
of the mordant?

And what did they think,
those who found
after your death,
all those untouched plates
of polished copper
on which to make the Passion?

The Puppet Master

He is perfectly visible
in his black cloak.

They say that after a while
you cease to notice him,
even though, like any puppeteer
he can kill
and bring to life again.

But it is not so.
Only when music plays
and he no longer speaks my lines
do I allow myself
to be dreamed.

The Voices

That day, they extolled
the cleverness of animals,
the glozing tongue
of the lion.

As I scaled his enclosure
I saw how he was
curiously furnished
with springs.

If caught
in the machinery,
he would cradle my head
in his jaws.

Song without voices

(for Los niños desaparacidos)

What is a pietà
without the body,
Christ the colourist
without the very
blood?

The poet in search of a voice

Listen!
the moon rustles the pasture,
a deer's foot splays the moss

and in that moment
of magical inattention
the words come

unpurposed, importunate,
acrobats, improvising
within a fall.

Acrobats at Rest

We are voyeurs
as they slump at the ringside
in their melancholy spangles.

Have they forgotten
how they forged up
the ladder of mild-steel

throats escutcheoned
like swallows
against the pitch of the tent

rib-cages sprung
with light
as the lasers fluoresced?

And was it nonchalance
or jeopardy
aerating the blood

while below,
not looking up,
a boy played with a marmoset?

The Green Harpsicord

Magisterial
the counterpoint
between bliss and presage.

How else
could we lift the lid
of the green harpsicord

to gilded flowers
and song-birds
in an open grave?

Glenn Gould at the virginals

On either side of midnight
the crape-myrtles sicken,
the sidewalks blue as hyssop
under a wolf moon.

He plays the Elizabethans
like crazy through the small hours,
the sweet gum trees
taking up the *rubato*.

Fantasias flow like prophets
and at the back of daylight
the sun makes a sound
on rising.

The Kindling

It is St Luke's little summer
and men are laying cables
across the wetlands.

They find a fuselage
in the peat, the pilot
still in the cockpit.

How it fuels the heart –
the centuries of pollen,
the deterioration of sugars

the windscreen wired
with thinnest layers of gold,
the mosses so green they simmer.

The Inspiriting

The white tree
is silence, parting
like many waters.

What kindles the trance
a flock of waxwings
alighting

their continuous song
an extension of the wind
in the branches

petals falling
with slow vertigo
and time not passing.

Herons

I saw them at first light,
the water throwing back
their bladed stillness,
nests half-hidden
in the rising mist.

Multiple exposure,
gauze on a grave presence;
and when they struck,
the ripple, like snow,
impossible to mislay.

Karumi

Early January,
snow falling without wind,
the hidden presence
of water beyond,
a white owl circling.

Any number of vanishing points:
capillary crystal,
high purity pounced with blood,
the spectral edge
between deepening and dispersal.

The North Face

At this altitude,
high winds reduce
the depth of snow on the dead.

Here, where they were last glimpsed,
film and camera
are disinterred,

the undeveloped dark
not whether they died
on the descent

but the keen light
along the sharp ascending ridge
before the cloud rolled in.

Slippage

It's a nice balance:
the climbers roped,
Himalayan ravens
rising from the valley.

When powder snow
leaves a vacuum
they are swept
into the zone

but never master
that other slippage –
curiosity
at riding the avalanche

while arresting ropes
burn to the bone.

At a remove

They bury the emperor
with his microscope
in the frozen drizzle

Shinto priests,
stockinged
over standing water

the banners swallow-tailed,
coffin triply sealed
on a tasselled palanquin

the paparazzi jostling –
their lens the only glass
to let blood

without bruising.

The Official Observer

Hiroshima 1945

We did not dream the rayographs
like a frieze of gods
along the wall

birds consecrated into carbon,
the spotted eagle
with a ball of myrrh

Dante's rose inverted
over the burning river
on the Feast of Transfiguration

but an official observer
above the kneeling city –
surely *this* we dreamed?

Gyrfalcon

She came through sea-mist
trailing jesses,
her whiteness flecked
with ermine.

I waste nothing
of how she braced herself
against the space
between words

the light as linguist,
that syllable in the blood
when she turned
on a lazy axle

in the eye of the wind.

The Flight of Icarus

*'What happens to the molecules is one thing: what
happens in the onlooker is less calculable by far.'*
FRANCIS SPUFFORD

How long did it last?
And is it still going on
for those who look up
from the lawn
with the kings and angels?

He is the sun's whipping-boy
flying into
the unseizable sign
which says
Deepen me.

Paint him
with raised brush-strokes
impasto –
all the big cats
kill with a neckbite.

And this particular body
this wax
that gives out a sound
if you tap it
with your knuckles

Look up –
unio mystica
where he catches the light
like a gilt shroud-pin
under the vapour trails

the gold hawk
with glass inlay,
etched on the zenith
like a clove
of Paradise.

As he suckles
he hears
the maternal heartbeat
in the background,
engine and ichor

the *duende*
of great sunlight
smoking the wax
until it runs
like anointing oil.

Which goldsmith
cast the sun
in a single piece
when he is fletched
with so many tongues

dropping seven skins
like a salamander,
as if he could
reassemble himself
before sundown?

in such a multitudinous falling
we expect sound
a winch to lower the angels,
the hiss of saltpetre
from undersea scars

the sky repeated
exactly in the water,
the sun's hawser
burning his hands
to the bone.

It fools the eye –
the discerning gesture –
the error on red
that makes an art
of bearing pain.

The Inexpressible Isle

Bright and howling
above the lugubrious swell
of the kelp beds

drowsing, like
a leopard of serenity
held on a purple cord.

A sunlit quay,
ships so stripped
they are visionary

fish with luminous bacteria
in pockets
under their eyes

fossils on the sea-bed
contorted in great calm,
vertigo

a diver removing his helmet,
the albatross still bolted
to the submerged mast.

Pouring the sand mandala into the Thames

I still hear them –
the Buddhist monks
rasping their cones
of coloured sand

the mandala falling
in a fine stream,
the river wearing
its oiled silks.

It forces the flow –
the treachery of images –
the briar that blooms
as if unpremeditated

then bewilders the bone.

Blizzard

In my dream
the landscape moved
with the mill

the air dark with flying meal,
refining drums spinning
their white silk

men working like pistons
to brake the sails
and through the shutters

hiss of snow
hushing
the hot millwheel.

Hoy

Mountain hares whiten.
Is it moonlight
or the blue shadow in snow?

The Colony

How they run
from the island laboratory,
the albino rabbits.

The dew falls on their whiteness
as if they are filmed
with the moistness of the moon

zinc white, titanium white,
their breath hanging
on the salt air.

They graze right up to
the metal cradles
swilling with chlorine, phosgene

and then they breed,
whitely, whitely
under the crumbling cement

through each soft winter.

The Asbestos Room

Here, the birds
no longer filch
soft-blue fibres
to line their nests
in the rafters.

Engines idle,
red coughs rise,
but the factory inspectors
admit to no shadow
on the lung.

How is it, in Sanskrit
there's no single word
for *breath*:
only the sounds for ingoing
and outgoing?

The Carrier Pigeon

(after Puvis de Chavannes)

On the tenement roof
a girl cups a carrier pigeon
to her breast,
as if wound to wound.

Nothing to staunch
the falcon above the walkway
but that immaculate
exchange.

Potosí

The moon falls
like a metaphysician
on the silver city

so distressed a metal –
even the horses shod with silver
in the freezing streets

wagons, blue with graffiti
under the spoil-tips,
and at first light

mountain foxes,
red as cinnabar,
moving against the flow

between the silver-bearing lodes,
the upland snow.

Robert Louis Stevenson dreams of Orkney in Samoa

Last night
a wind came over the sea,
keen as a swan's bone,
particular with the dead.

I saw my father
and grandfather, inspecting
the major lighthouses
as the skerries smoked by.

Here, azure orchids burn,
kingfishers refract
the great white light –
but for a moment

I weigh the examined life,
the necessary exile,
against the way light behaves
between islands.

The Lightkeeper

Whenever I taste salt
on my skin
I remember
the lightkeeper's room

high up a spiral stair
under the lantern,
revolving beams
sweeping the white night.

You – telling me
of other lighthouses,
sundials from Cape Wrath
and Sule Skerry

the little door flung open
onto the balcony,
its brass rail
gathering the horizon

below, an overgrown garden,
a small graveyard,
sea-swallows between us
and the shingle

the wind gusting,
our bodies braced suddenly
with silk cords
against the spindrift.

Salt over Skara Brae

(for Elizabeth Scarth)

I

It is not the sea-wind –
that salt in the eye
is sister and brother

under the heather
the dead are spring-heeled,
sand blown from the vertebrae

there is spruce on the shore
rafter of whale-rib,
bedding of blue clay

surf on the lintel
hazelnut shells,
elkskin and scapula

stones heat the water,
glistening lovers
run to red ochre

Queen of Peace –
put the salt-white host
on your tongue.

II

You brought stones patiently by boat
from midden and burnt mound;
volcanic stones,
quernstone and hollowed mortar,
stones from the recess in the scullery
which once housed the goose on her nest;
dropped them into the shallow loch
till the small island rose
and reflected meadowsweet
seeded the dusk.

Even now
from the high white drawing-room
I see you standing in freshwater
but looking seaward;
behind you, such shimmering replay,
I am not sure whether
the standing stones over the horizon
lean a moment into the wind,
or whether their shadows kneel
between waters.

III

Not unaccompanied burial –
under Scapa Flow
fish graze the guns
of the scuttled fleet,
the sea wears
the helicopter's circles
like a talismanic shirt;
below the swell,
heavy cups hang
in deepwater rows
from the ceiling of the serving room.

In the flare
above the blockship,
the *Hindenberg* lifts
from her bed
of compressed oil;
cormorants are runes on the rigging;
along the causeway
where the herring-shoals
once flashed,
fossil-fish mouth
from their several horizons.

How the whale-oil burns
with its wick of rush-pith;
and from the chapel
on Flotta,
the lit impulse
of the lost altar –
the tear-drop
shaped like a flame –
as if, above the open sea-hatches,
angels still freshen
with transcendence.

IV

This is the sung mass:
slingstones
for the songbirds of Quanterness

the white-tailed sea eagle
stripping flesh
before burial

a carved footprint
on the threshold
as rite for the limbless

the libation of the tribe
antler, young otter,
whole fish from inland water

a scattered necklace
where the freshly dead
sample exposure

how articulate –
the crimsoning ancestry,
the uneaten lamb in the tomb –

prisoners of war
bartering for meat
their model-ships of bone.

V

We were too late to take the causeway

but the hinterland is tidal,
the whole island in stormtime
washed by sea-water;

salt on the smelting-hearth,
silver cones
in a larch casket.

Our luminous hoard
the erosion of horizons
from low isles

to recover from the sandspit
the surgeon's lancet
the jaw of the porpoise

unset sapphires,
a spice-box of speckled jade –
against the incoming tide

a glimpse of the mainland.

VI

*'Sir John Franklin sailed from Stromness in 1845, seeking
the North West Passage, having watered at Login's Well.'*

No anchorage
eluded them –
only an alert from the crow's nest,
search-vessels
at the vanishing point.

The sledging party
have scurvy;
John Torrington wears
the blue wool
from the coffin lid.

The unmelting dead
still plot
their opaque passage
in the ship's library
under blankets of wolfskin;

but it flows through the permafrost –
their blue derangement –
the well
and the watering,
the imperfect lead solder.

VII

Such argosy –
the sunk merchantman
with cabins of sandalwood
in the brushed cobalt;
saltpetre and squirrel-pelt,
ivory gull and porcelain crab
on cannon under the kelp.

The sound is watered silk,
the sea foiled
by white sand
to simulate emerald;
that spume on the causeway
scrimshaw and crucible,
muslin from Bengal.

At no depth
are the drowned silenced.
Deliverance is watermarked;
a candle
of beachcomber's wax
still bleeds
for the maiden voyage.

VIII

*'and on the thirteenth day of Christmas they travelled
on foot over to Firth. During a snowstorm they took
shelter in Maeshowe and there two of them went insane...'*
ORKNEYINGA SAGA

Mercy is unseasonable –
pilgrims glimmer
through the sleet,
the skull
a bone lantern.

The delirious
glimpse longships
in the blizzard,
the winter king and queen
departing for the hunt.

Blue virgin –
those who go to Byzantium
take no treasure
redder
then Pentecost.

Holiness hones –
over Jerusalem
slim blades
crimsoning
the solstice.

Red Christ
in the white mound –
this is the surgery
of light
*they came unto the sepulchre
at the rising of the sun.*

IX

We made such calm departures –
salt on the causeway,
rigging bleached by the wind;
jellyfish gliding past
like lampshades under the swell.

We did not ask
if sun or cymbal
burnished the silence,
cloudscape or coastline
receded with the seal singing;

and as for inland music –
we remembered none
except the rustling field
of the cloth of gold where
the warrior is buried with glass bowls.

But with hindsight,
we should have seen by the light
through the flint arrowhead,
borne dangerous cargoes,
burned to the waterline.